AMERICAN HUMANE

Protecting Children & Animals Since 1877

Top 10 Cats for Kids

Dana Meachen Rau

Enslow Elementary

an imprint of

Enslow Publishers, Inc.
40 Industrial Road
Box 398
Berkeley Heights, NJ 07922
USA

http://www.enslow.com

AMERICAN HUMANE

Protecting Children & Animals Since 1877

Founded in 1877, the American Humane Association is the oldest national organization dedicated to protecting both children and animals. Through a network of child and animal protection agencies and individuals, the American Humane Association develops policies, legislation, curricula, and training programs to protect children and animals from abuse, neglect, and exploitation. To learn how you can support the vision of a nation where no child or animal will ever be a victim of willful abuse or neglect, visit www.americanhumane.org, phone (303) 792-9900, or write to the American Humane Association at 63 Inverness Drive East, Englewood, Colorado, 80112-5117.

Enslow Elementary, an imprint of Enslow Publishers, Inc.

Enslow Elementary® is a registered trademark of Enslow Publishers, Inc.

Library of Congress Cataloging-in-Publication Data
Rau, Dana Meachen, 1971–
  Top 10 cats for kids / Dana Meachen Rau.
    p. cm. — (Top Pets for Kids with American Humane)
  Summary: "Provides facts on the top ten cat breeds for kids and how to care for them"—Provided by publisher.
  Includes bibliographical references and index.
  ISBN-13: 978-0-7660-3071-8
  ISBN-10: 0-7660-3071-7
  1. Cat breeds—Juvenile literature. 2. Cats—Juvenile literature.
I. Title. II. Title: Top ten cats for kids.
  SF445.7.R37 2008
  636.8—dc22

                                    2007024440

Printed in the United States of America

10 9 8 7 6 5 4 3

To Our Readers:
We have done our best to make sure that all Internet Addresses in this book were active and appropriate when we went to press. However, the author and publisher have no control over and assume no liability for the material available on those Internet sites or on other Web sites they may link to. Any comments or suggestions can be sent by e-mail to comments@enslow.com or to the address on the back cover.

♻ Enslow Publishers, Inc., is committed to printing our books on recycled paper. The paper in every book contains 10% to 30% post-consumer waste (PCW). The cover board on the outside of each book contains 100% PCW. Our goal is to do our part to help young people and the environment too!

Cover Photo: Alan Robinson/Ron Kimball Stock
Interior Photos: Alamy/Juniors Bildarchiv, pp. 8, 32 left; Alamy/dk, p. 10; Alamy/Petra Wegner, p. 41; Animals Animals—Earth Scenes/Ulrike Schanz, p. 36; Animals Animals—Earth Scenes/Werner Layer, p. 39; Associated Press, pp. 17 bottom, 32 right; iStockphoto.com/Michael Chen, p. 1; iStockphoto.com/Mehmet Salih Guler, pp. 2, 44; iStockphoto.com/Oleg Prikhodko, p. 4; iStockphoto.com/HTuller, pp. 5, 9, 19, 43; iStockphoto.com/Carmen Martínez Banús, p. 18; iStockphoto.com/Victor Soares, p. 21; iStockphoto.com/Shelly Perry, p. 42; iStockphoto.com/Debi Bishop, p. 45; iStockphoto.com/Ira Bachinskaya, p. 46; iStockphoto.com/Larisa Lofitskaya, p. 47; iStockphoto.com/Alex Bramwell, p. 48; Jupiter Images/Comstock, pp. 15, 16; Ron Kimball Stock/Ron Kimball, pp. 6, 7, 13, 17 top, 23, 24, 27, 28, 30, 38, 40; Ron Kimball Stock/Alan Robinson, pp. 22, 26, 34, 37; Amy Williams, pp. 3, 35.

The top 10 cats are approved by the American Humane Association and are listed alphabetically.

Contents

So You Want to Get a Cat?

All cats are different, just like all people are different. Some cats like lots of attention from their owners. Your cat might always be rubbing against your leg, or even sitting on your homework so that you pay attention to her instead. But other cats like to be alone. You might only see your cat for meals. The rest of the

◀ Cats are very popular as pets. One reason is because they are often independent, but make great companions.

▲

Whether yours is shy, or friendly and cuddly, living with any cat is always interesting!

time, she might be under a bed, in a corner, or exploring the house. If you decide to get a cat, you have to be ready for anything!

Sometimes your cat might remind you of a wild cat. He might lie on the top of the refrigerator like it is a tree. He might try to hunt mice in the garage. Just like a lion waits in the tall grass to pounce on a zebra, your cat might wait behind a chair to pounce on you!

But pet cats are not wild animals. They need love and care from people to live. They need to be fed and brushed. They need lots of attention.

Before you get a cat, you and your family need to think about several things. Do you have time to take care of a cat? Do you already have other pets, and if so, will they get along with a new one? Does anyone in your house have allergies? If you go on vacation, do you know someone who can come in to feed your cat? Cats can live for 15 to 20 years. Are you ready to be a friend to a cat for her whole life?

▲

Like all pets, cats need plenty of love, attention, and care.

7

How to Have a Healthy Cat

One of your main jobs will be to feed your cat. Your veterinarian (vet) will let you know which kind of food your cat should eat. Your cat also needs to drink clean water. Make sure he has plenty of water to drink at all times.

Have special food and water bowls for your cat. Cats need to be fed about two

◄ Your vet can tell you what kind of food is best for your cat. Be sure that your cat always has fresh water to drink!

times a day. Kittens need to be fed three or four times a day. Wash out the food and water bowls with warm, soapy water, then rinse them clean. You should do this after each meal or at the end of each day.

Grooming

You do not have to give your cat a bath. Cats clean themselves by licking their fur with their scratchy tongues. But doing this causes them to swallow some of the hair. Swallowing too much can cause hairballs. Hairballs can get stuck in a cat's stomach, causing her to vomit. Gently brushing your cat's hair with a special brush can help get rid of excess hair. If your cat has short hair, you need to brush her only once a week. If you have a long-haired cat, you might need to do it every day. Most cats enjoy brushing because they like the attention.

Litter Box

Cats go to the bathroom in a litter box. You should put your cat's litter box in a quiet place away from her food area. Every day, you need to scoop out the cat's waste and throw it in the trash. Once a week, you need to empty all of the litter out of the box and discard it in the trash. Next, wash the box with warm, soapy water, and put in new litter. Whenever you scoop out waste or change litter, you must wash your hands thoroughly with soap and warm water afterward.

Most cats will know how to use the litter box without being shown. Kittens learn by watching their mothers. But if a kitten has not yet learned, you may have to show him. To do this, put him in the litter box when he wakes up from sleeping, or a few times during the day. He will soon learn that the litter box is where he should go to the bathroom.

Teaching Your Cat

Cats might try to explore places you do not want them to go. If your cat jumps up on the kitchen counter, you can take her off and say "no." If you do this over and over again you may be able to teach her not to go there. Never hit or hurt your cat. You should always be gentle. That way, when you say "no," your cat will trust you and be more likely to listen.

Even so, you may not be able to stop some behaviors.

You can prevent trouble by giving your cat better choices. If your cat likes to climb, you can get him a cat tree. To keep your cat from scratching the furniture, give him a tall scratching post. Try moving him to it whenever he tries to scratch something he should not. You can keep a box of cat toys where he can reach them. That way, he will be less tempted to go somewhere he should not. When your cat does something good, you can give him a cat treat as a reward.

▲

Try rewarding your cat when he uses his scratching post. He will be more likely to use it again and again.

Safety

You should keep your cat indoors, because that is the safest place for him. However, even your home has some dangers. For example, some houseplants can make cats very sick or even kill them if they are eaten. Ask your vet for a list of these plants. Then, either get rid of the plants or put them where your cat cannot reach them.

Also be sure to pick up small objects so your cat cannot choke on them. These might include rubber bands or scraps of yarn or string. Lock household cleaners in cabinets. Make sure window screens are secure so your cat will not fall out if she sits on the windowsill.

Health Care

Keep your cat healthy by bringing him to a vet for regular checkups. Before you even bring your new cat home, you should have a vet picked out. At a regular checkup, a vet will weigh your cat, take his temperature, and check his skin and coat, eyes, and ears. Your cat will need vaccinations so that he does not get diseases.

▲

Regular trips to the vet are important for keeping your cat healthy. Bring a list of questions for the vet each time you go.

If your cat is sick, the vet might give you medicine that you need to give your cat at home.

Your vet will suggest that you have your cat spayed (female cats) or neutered (male cats). These operations are performed so that cats cannot produce kittens. This is good for your cat's health, and it will help prevent the birth of unwanted kittens.

Cat Supplies You Will Need:

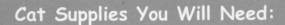

Crate

- Crate for trips to the vet
- Litter box
- Litter
- Litter scoop
- Food and water bowls

- Cat food (dry or wet)
- Cat bed (if you wish)
- Tall scratching post
- Toys
- Brush (or comb, for some long-haired cats)

If Your Cat Gets Lost

If your cat gets lost, you want to be sure whoever finds him will know he belongs to you. You can get a collar for your cat with an ID tag. The collar should be made of elastic, or be of the "breakaway"

All cats should wear a collar and an identification tag. ▶

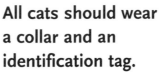

type, so your cat can slip out of it if the collar gets caught on something. You can

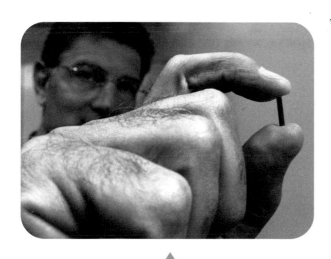

▲

One way to make sure your cat always has identification is to have a vet put a tiny microchip under your cat's skin.

also have a vet put a microchip just under your cat's skin. If he is lost and someone finds him, they can bring him to a vet. The vet can scan the microchip and see who the cat belongs to.

Choosing the Purrfect Pet

Do you want a cat or a kitten? Kittens are cute and playful. But they cannot be left alone all day. They are still learning about things, and they could hurt themselves if no one is there to watch out for them.

Grown-up cats are already used to being around people. They may not need as much attention.

◀ Many people want to adopt kittens. But there are lots of good reasons to adopt an adult cat.

Do you want a purebred cat or a mixed-breed cat? A purebred cat has been bred to look and act a certain way. For example, a Persian has long, flowing fur. A Siamese has lots of energy. There are between 80 and 100 breeds of cats. Mixed-breed cats are a mixture of many breeds.

The best place to get a mixed-breed cat is at an animal shelter. Shelters take in both kittens and older cats whose owners can no longer care for them. A cat from a shelter will not cost too much money to adopt.

Sometimes purebred cats can also be found at an animal shelter. Or you can go to a breeder to buy one. These are people who breed purebred cats and can prove that the parents were of the same breed. A purebred cat can cost hundreds of dollars.

One of a cat's favorite things is a comfortable, sunny place to stretch out!

Make sure you choose a healthy cat. A healthy cat will have bright eyes, clean ears, and pale pink gums and tongue. The cat's coat should be shiny. The cat should not be too skinny. Ask to play with the cat or kitten before you take her home. Is she friendly? Does she like to be held? Does she seem active and interested in you?

A kitten should not be adopted until he is at least eight to ten weeks old. Then he is ready to leave his mother.

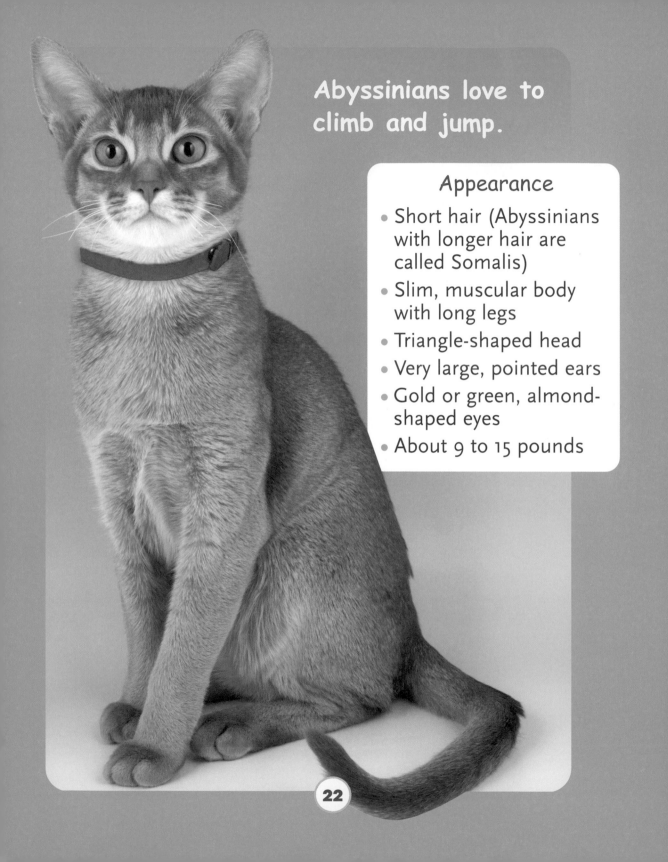

Abyssinians love to climb and jump.

Appearance

- Short hair (Abyssinians with longer hair are called Somalis)
- Slim, muscular body with long legs
- Triangle-shaped head
- Very large, pointed ears
- Gold or green, almond-shaped eyes
- About 9 to 15 pounds

Chapter 1

Abyssinian

This active, friendly breed is named after Abyssinia (now Ethiopia, a country in Africa), where people believed this type of cat lived long ago.

Color

Abyssinians have a ticked coat. This means that there are lines of darker color on each hair. The most common color is ruddy, which is brownish red with black ticking.

General Behavior

Abyssinians:
1. love to climb and jump.
2. are smart and curious and will check out anything you bring into the house.
3. will follow you around and want to play with you.
4. are quiet cats— they hardly ever use their voices.
5. are gentle and loving.

Special Needs

Abyssinians need lots of space, so they would not do well in a very small home.

◀ Active, smart, curious, and quiet are words that best describe an Abyssinian cat.

American shorthairs make loud purring sounds when happy.

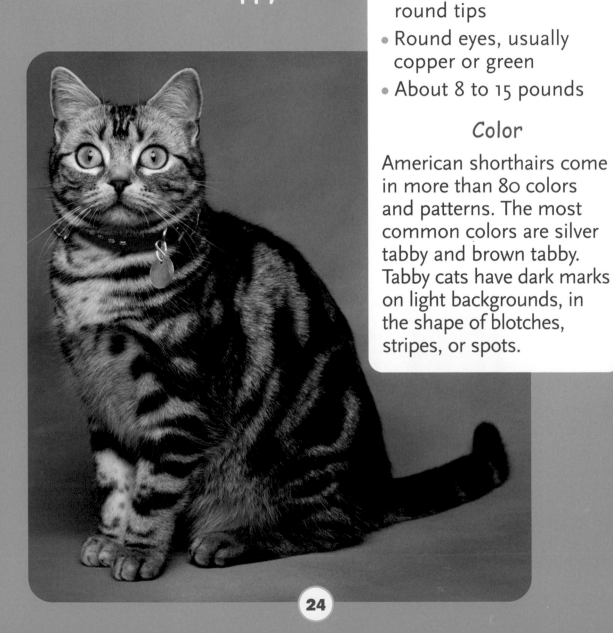

Appearance

- Short hair
- Muscular body
- Wide, full-cheeked face
- Medium-sized ears with round tips
- Round eyes, usually copper or green
- About 8 to 15 pounds

Color

American shorthairs come in more than 80 colors and patterns. The most common colors are silver tabby and brown tabby. Tabby cats have dark marks on light backgrounds, in the shape of blotches, stripes, or spots.

Chapter 2

American Shorthair

The first cats came to America on ships with European settlers in the 1600s. People often brought cats on ships to help keep the rats under control. Over time, cats became popular as pets. In the early 1900s, some breeders took some cats with qualities they liked and created a new breed. The breed was first called domestic shorthair. It is now called American shorthair, to set them apart from mixed-breed cats.

General Behavior

American shorthairs:

1. are friendly and playful, but also like to sit and watch.
2. make loud purring sounds when happy.
3. are full of energy, so they need lots of space.
4. are usually very healthy, and often live to 20 years or so.
5. are known for being good hunters, so they will catch mice and flies in the house.

Special Needs

American shorthairs like to eat a lot, so pay attention to how much your cat is fed, and make sure he gets exercise.

◄ Silver tabby is one of the most common color patterns for these energetic, healthy expert hunters.

Maine coons are very strong, and good hunters.

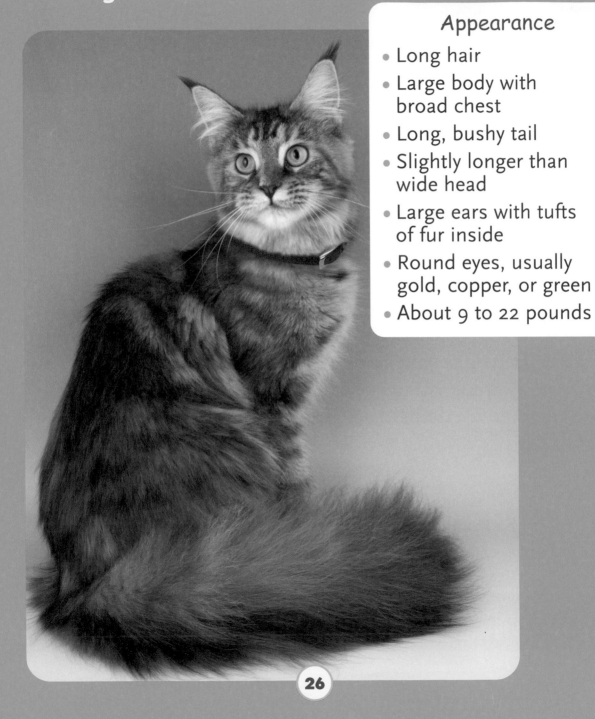

Appearance

- Long hair
- Large body with broad chest
- Long, bushy tail
- Slightly longer than wide head
- Large ears with tufts of fur inside
- Round eyes, usually gold, copper, or green
- About 9 to 22 pounds

Chapter 3

Maine Coon

Maine coons are named for the state where they were found, and for their raccoon-like bushy, ringed tails. They are the largest breed of pet cats.

Color

Maine coons come in many patterns and colors. The most common is brown tabby.

General Behavior

Maine coons:
1. are easygoing and friendly.
2. are very strong, and good hunters.
3. are very curious and like to play and climb.
4. do not mind big families and are friendly with other pets.
5. do not meow. Instead, they make a chirping noise.

Special Needs

A Maine coon's long coat needs to be groomed often to keep it from getting matted, or tangled, in thick knots.

◀ Always curious and looking for adventure—that is a Maine coon!

Manx like to play, and can be easily trained to do some tricks.

Appearance

- Short, thick hair (a Manx with longer hair is called a Cymric)
- Short, round body. Back legs are longer than front legs, so it sometimes looks like the cat is hopping.
- Round head
- Widely spaced ears
- Round eyes
- No tail or very short tail (Manx with no tail at all are called rumpies)
- About 8 to 12 pounds

Chapter 4

Manx

The first thing you might notice about a Manx cat is that it has a short stump for a tail, if it has any tail at all! Manx cats were first identified on the Isle of Man, an island off England's western coast.

Color

Manx come in many patterns and colors. The most common are tabby, calico, and tortoiseshell. Calico cats have larger patches of black and red and white. Tortoiseshell cats have black and red hair in patches.

General Behavior

Manx:
1. are mellow and relaxed.
2. like laps but do not always like high places, so they may not like to be carried.
3. like to play, and can be easily trained to do some tricks, such as fetching.
4. might pick a favorite member of the family, like dogs often do, and follow that person around.

Special Needs

Manx often like to play with shiny objects. Be careful not to leave out jewelry, paper clips, or other small, shiny items.

◀ A Manx is easy to pick out because it either has a very stubby tail, or no tail at all!

A mixed-breed cat might be friendly and love company.

Appearance

- Short or long hair
- Body can be round with short legs or slim with long legs, and anything in between
- Triangle-shaped or round head
- Pointed or rounded ears
- Almond, oval, or round-shaped eyes
- Wide range of weights, from about 6 to 15 pounds

Chapter 5

Mixed Breed

Want a truly special pet? Try a mixed-breed cat! Most pet cats are mixed-breed cats. These cats are a combination of many breeds. Every mixed-breed cat looks and acts different. Mixed-breed cats are often called domestic longhairs or domestic shorthairs.

Color

Mixed-breed cats come in many colors, such as black, red, brown, cream, and white. They can have many patterns on their coats. Bicolor cats are one color on the top and white on the legs and belly.

General Behavior

A mixed-breed cat might be friendly and love company. Or she might be shy and hide when someone comes over to visit. She might be nonstop action and full of energy. Or she might like to lie in a sunny spot and watch while you play.

Special Needs

Since mixed-breed cats are so different from one another, it will be an adventure as you get to know your pet and learn about his individual needs. Your vet will let you know if your cat has any special health concerns.

◄ Any mixed-breed cat is truly one-of-a-kind. They each have their own special look and "personality."

Persians love to be petted and sit on laps.

Appearance

- Long hair
- Short, broad body with short legs
- Very round, flat face
- Short tail with bushy hair
- Small, round-tipped ears
- Round eyes, which are copper, dark orange, green, or blue
- About 8 to 15 pounds

Color

Persians come in more than 50 different colors and patterns.

Chapter 6

Persian

Persians are the most popular purebred pet cat in the world. Long-haired cats that became known as "Persians" started in Turkey and Iran (once known as Persia).

Special Needs

A Persian cat needs to be combed every single day. Otherwise, the fur will get matted, and combing out this knotted hair can be painful for the cat. Because of their flat faces, they may need to have the fur around their eyes cleaned regularly.

General Behavior

Persians:

1. are not energetic and will spend most of the day lying around watching what is going on.
2. hardly ever jump or climb.
3. have a very quiet voice that they hardly use.
4. love to be petted and sit on laps.
5. are very gentle and like to cuddle.
6. do not mind lots of action going on around them, but they might not join in.

◀ Gentle and cuddly with soft, long fur—it is easy to see why Persians are so popular!

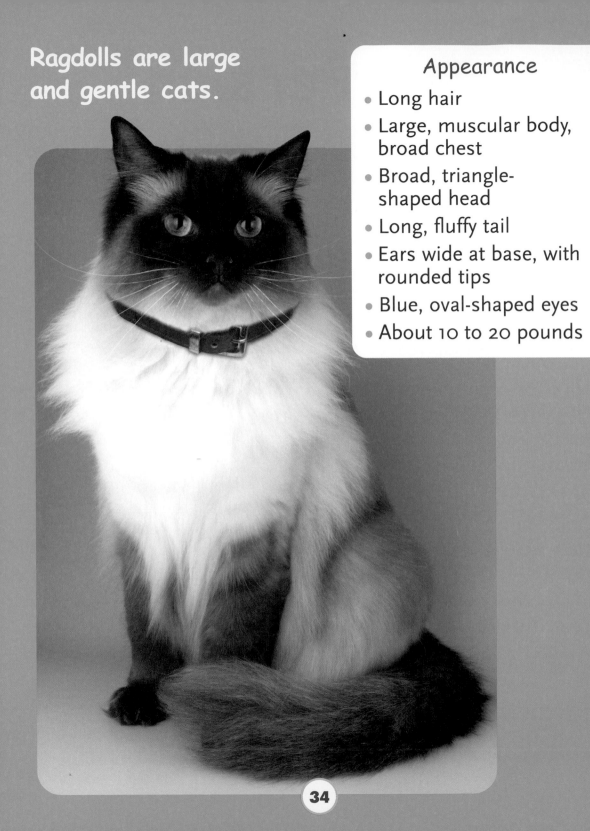

Ragdolls are large and gentle cats.

Appearance

- Long hair
- Large, muscular body, broad chest
- Broad, triangle-shaped head
- Long, fluffy tail
- Ears wide at base, with rounded tips
- Blue, oval-shaped eyes
- About 10 to 20 pounds

Chapter 7

Ragdoll

The ragdoll breed gets its name from the fact that when you pick one up, the cat tends to go limp, like a rag doll.

Color

Ragdolls can be bicolor, pointed, or mitted. Mitted means they have white "mitts" on their paws. Pointed cats have light bodies and dark faces, ears, tails, and feet.

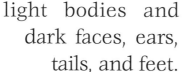

General Behavior

Ragdolls:
1. are large and gentle cats.
2. are very quiet and do not meow often.
3. like people and are very friendly with their owners and visitors.
4. are not very active or energetic, but will be playful.

Special Needs

Ragdolls have long hair, but it does not mat as much as other long-haired breeds. They do not need to be groomed daily, but should be combed once a week.

◄ Ragdolls may be quiet, but they are friendly and like to have fun!

Russian blues are quiet
cats who like quiet houses.

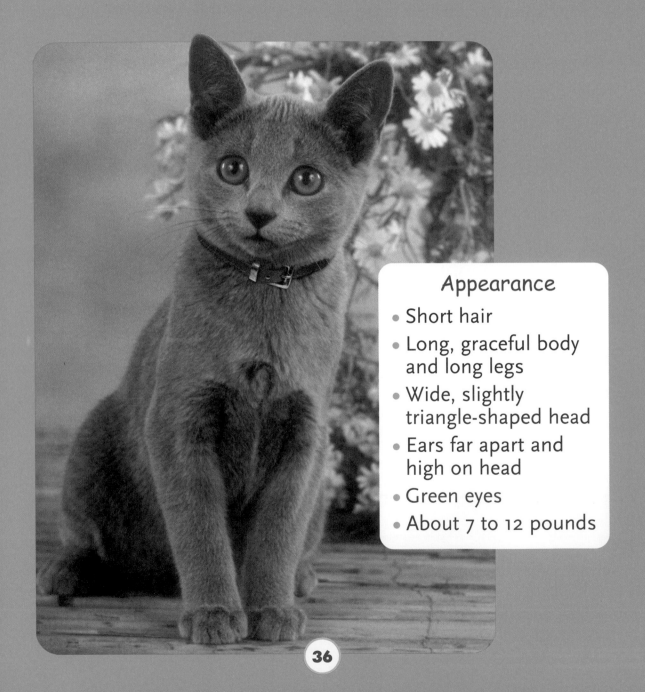

Appearance

- Short hair
- Long, graceful body and long legs
- Wide, slightly triangle-shaped head
- Ears far apart and high on head
- Green eyes
- About 7 to 12 pounds

Chapter 8

Russian Blue

Russian blues are named for the country where they were first found, and for their unique bluish-gray color.

General Behavior

Russian blues:

1. are quiet cats who like quiet houses.
2. may be scared of visitors and run and hide when people come to your house.
3. are very gentle and loving with their owners.
4. can be energetic and playful, but will not get into too much trouble.

Special Needs

Russian blues have short, very thick hair. It should be brushed twice a week.

◄ A quiet, shy, and loving Russian blue can make a great companion to have around the house.

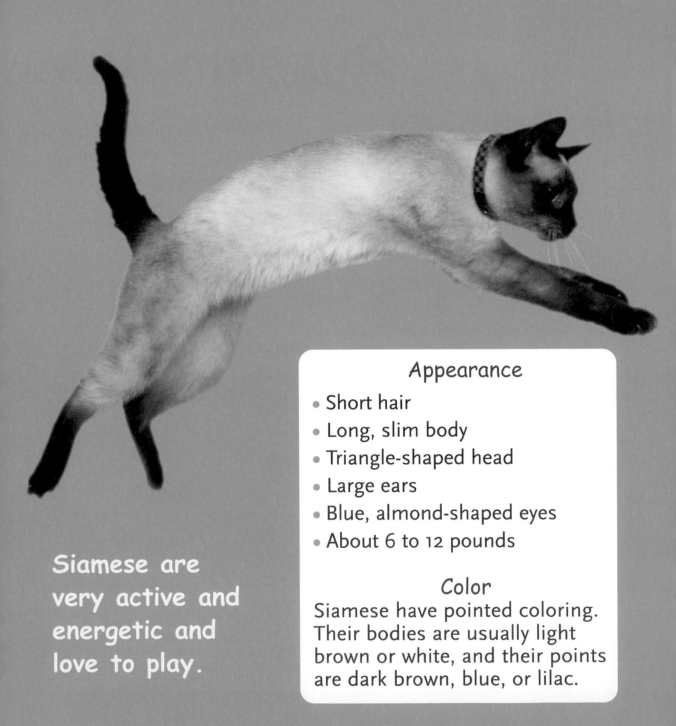

Siamese are
very active and
energetic and
love to play.

Appearance

- Short hair
- Long, slim body
- Triangle-shaped head
- Large ears
- Blue, almond-shaped eyes
- About 6 to 12 pounds

Color

Siamese have pointed coloring.
Their bodies are usually light
brown or white, and their points
are dark brown, blue, or lilac.

Siamese

Do you want lots of action? Do you want a cat that "talks" a lot? Bring home a Siamese cat! This breed originally came from Thailand, which was once called Siam.

Special Needs

Siamese need a lot of attention and space to play because they have so much energy.

General Behavior

Siamese:

1. are very active and energetic and love to play.
2. are very smart and curious. They like to know what you are doing and may follow you around the house.
3. like to sit on laps, be held, and also be carried around.
4. are known for being very talkative. Their voices are loud, and they meow a lot!

◀ Siamese are the stunt people of the cat world—always ready for action!

39

Tonkinese are energetic, active, and can get into trouble.

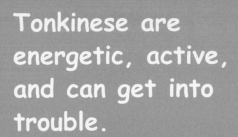

Appearance

- Short hair
- Slim like Siamese, but heavier than you would expect for their size
- Triangle-shaped head
- Large ears
- Aqua-colored, almond-shaped eyes
- About 6 to 12 pounds

Chapter 10

Tonkinese

Tonkinese cats are so active and curious that it might be a good idea to have two of them. They can keep each other company, and out of trouble! This breed was created by mixing Siamese and Burmese cats.

Color

Tonkinese have pointed coloring in brown, cream, blue, and gray.

General Behavior

Tonkinese:
1. like to have company and attention.
2. are very curious.
3. are energetic, active, and can get into trouble.
4. like to sit on laps.
5. are not as talkative as Siamese, but still very vocal.

Special Needs

Tonkinese are very active and need a lot of room and attention. Have lots of toys to keep them busy when you are out.

◄ Having a Tonkinese is like living with a friend who always wants to play.

Bringing Your New Cat Home

The first day home with your new pet can be exciting. But you have to be patient. Start by keeping your cat in one room with everything she needs. After a few days, open the door and let her explore. If you have other pets, they need to get to know your new cat, too. Do not leave another cat or dog alone with your new cat for the first few days.

◀ Before you know it, your new pet will be as comfortable in your home as any other member of the family!

43

Kittens are naturally curious about other animals. On the other hand, it will take older animals a little time to get used to newcomers.

A safe way to introduce your pets to each other is by having your new cat in a crate when your pets first meet. Watch how they react to each other. If one of them acts fearful or aggressive, separate them and keep them apart. Let them meet again, little by little, over time, with the new cat in the crate each time. When they act relaxed and appear comfortable together, let your new cat out of the crate. It might take as long as two weeks for your pets to accept each other as part of the family.

Within the first week of getting your cat, you should bring her to the vet for a checkup. The vet will make sure your cat has all of her shots and is healthy. And the doctor will be able to give you tips on taking care of your new family member.

Your cat will depend on you to give him all the things he needs, including food and shelter. But the love and attention you give him is just as important.

Lots of love is just as important for a pet cat as food and shelter.

Glossary

allergies—Physical reactions (including coughing or sneezing) that are caused by a certain source, such as an animal.

animal shelter—A place where people can adopt animals that other people can no longer care for.

breeder—A person who breeds purebred cats, which are bred to look and act a certain way.

cat tree—A climbing toy made just for cats.

matted—Tangled into thick knots.

neutered—When male cats have the organs removed that help them produce kittens.

spayed—When female cats have the organs removed that help them produce kittens.

ticked—A type of animal hair that has lines of darker color on each hair.

vaccination—A shot that gives a pet medications that prevent harmful diseases.

veterinarian (vet)—A doctor who takes care of animals.

Further Reading

Crisp, Marty. *Everything Cat: What Kids Really Want to Know About Cats.* Chanhassen, Minn.: NorthWord Press, 2003.

Dennis-Bryan, Kim. *Kitten Care: A Guide to Loving and Nurturing Your Pet.* New York: Dorling Kindersley, 2004.

Gunter, Veronika Alice, and Rain Newcomb. *Pet Science: 50 Purr-fectly Woof-Worthy Activities for You and Your Pets.* New York: Lark Books, 2006.

Jones, Annie. *All About Cats.* New York: Chelsea House, 2005.

Ring, Susan. *Caring for Your Cat.* Mankato, Minn.: Weigl Publishers Inc., 2003.

Internet Addresses

American Humane Association
http://www.americanhumane.org

ASPCA: Animaland
http://www.animaland.org

The Cat Fancier's Association
http://www.cfa.org/index.html

Index